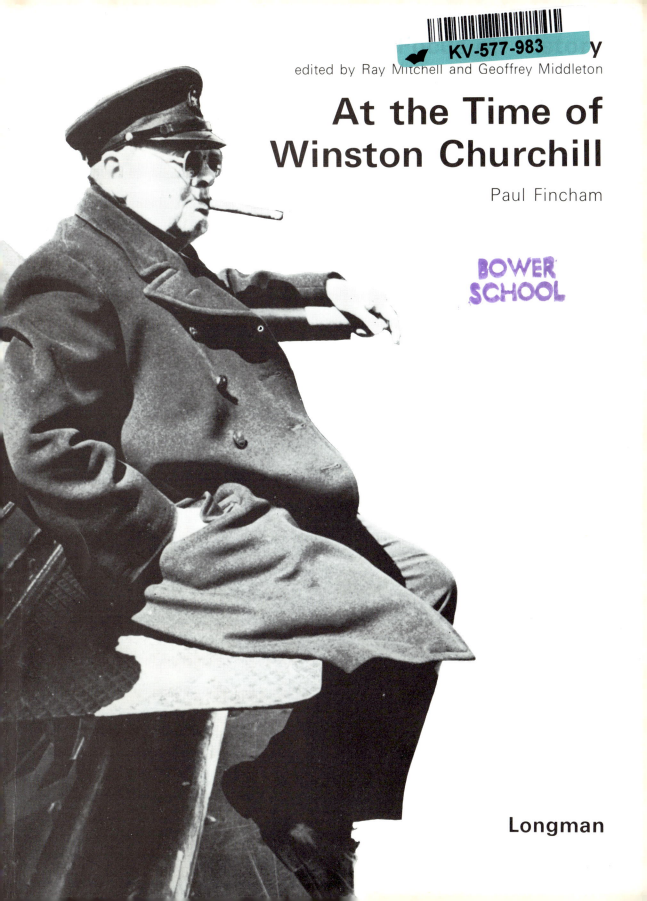

edited by Ray Mitchell and Geoffrey Middleton

# At the Time of Winston Churchill

Paul Fincham

**Longman**

This is not the life story of Winston Churchill, but the story of life in his time. When he was born, Queen Victoria ruled over the British Empire. Life has changed more since then than during any other period in our history. Some of these changes are described in this book. The list of contents will give you an idea of what you will find here.

## List of contents

# The world of the rich

This great house, Blenheim Palace in Oxfordshire, was built for John Churchill, 1st Duke of Marlborough. It was named after the battle of Blenheim, where the duke beat the French in 1704.

On 30th November 1874, a boy was born there — Winston Spencer Churchill. He was fortunate in being born into a rich and noble family. His father, whom you can see on the souvenir plate below, was Lord Randolph Churchill, a son of the 7th Duke of Marlborough. Winston's mother was a beautiful American lady, Jennie Jerome.

Winston was 2 years old when this photograph was taken of him with her. Notice how small children wore frocks even if they were boys. He later said of his mother, 'She shone for me like the evening star.'

LORD RANDOLPH CHURCHILL,
CHANCELLOR OF THE EXCHEQUER.
1886

When Winston was serving as a young soldier in India, at the age of 21, he heard people there singing this song:

'Great White Mother, far across the sea,
Ruler of the Empire may she ever be,
Long may she reign, glorious and free.'

The 'Great White Mother' of the song was Queen Victoria. Her empire was those lands which Britain governed, or helped to govern. It covered nearly one quarter of the world. You can see the empire (the shaded areas) on this Canadian stamp. Look for the crown and read the words under the map.

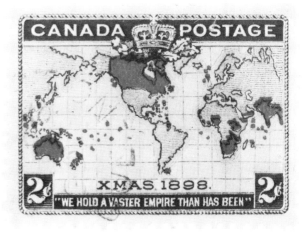

Britain was proud of the empire. Most of the colonies have become independent since then, and now rule themselves, but at that time businessmen and investors earned millions of pounds from them.

Queen Victoria's birthday, 24th May, was celebrated as Empire Day. Schoolchildren lined up to salute the Union Jack, then had a day's holiday. In this photograph of the Empire Day festivities in a small country town, find these things:
— the headmaster, with cap and gown, on the platform
— two boys standing guard over the flagpole. You can see the base of it under the tree
— the children all wearing their best clothes
— one boy already practising his salute.

In 1901, after ruling for 64 years, Queen Victoria died. Her son succeeded her and became King Edward VII. The 10 years of his reign are known as the 'Edwardian Age'.

If you were rich in the Edwardian Age, life was comfortable. Above are the servants of a large country house. Count how many there are. Some are 'indoor' and some 'outdoor' servants. Try to decide which are which. Find the housekeeper, seated in the centre, wearing a cap. She ran the house and organised the other servants. Can you pick out: the chef, the head butler and the head gardener?

The girls in white are housemaids. What kind of work do you think is done by those boys sitting in front?

There were fewer jobs for women then, so girls often 'went into service' which means they went to work as servants for other families. In 1891 it was estimated that 1 in every 3 girls between the ages of 15 and 20 was in domestic service. A housemaid might earn £20 a year. She worked long hours, but had a good home and nourishing food. Girls in service were sometimes able to send home a little money, or some clothes, to help other members of their families.

In those days before the First World War, the 'upper classes' in English society amused themselves with weekend parties at large country houses, like Blenheim Palace.

At these parties rich people gossiped, danced, played games and cards, and ate enormous meals. Look at the picture above of a correctly laid breakfast table of this time and pick out:

- the folded napkins made of linen
- boiled eggs in a special egg-stand
- silver dishes with covers. These held bacon, sausages, kidneys and several sorts of fish
- the teapot and the kettle with its own little spirit-lamp to keep the water hot.

Compare all this with your breakfast today. What are some of the differences? Remember, there were servants to set the table, clean the silver and wash the cloths and napkins.

This menu for a royal luncheon is a fairly simple one. Some people ate much more than this. Find Queen Victoria's initial and the picture of Windsor Castle. Why was part of the menu written in French? You may be able to translate some of it.

THE ROYAL LUNCHEON,
Tuesday, 2nd July, 1895

Potage, Beau Veau
Œufs à la Villeroi
Côtelettes d'Agneau panées et sautées
Ris de Veau au riz
Poulets sautés aux truffes
Asperges à la sauce

Hot and Cold Roast Fowls
Cold Tongue.   Cold Roast Beef
Galantine de Volaille
Homard au naturel, sauce Remoulade

Pouding Diplomate, sauce aux fraises
Parfait à la Victoria

Dinner was at 8.30 pm. Afterwards the hostess led her lady guests to the 'withdrawing room' and the gentlemen settled down to drink port wine. What are some of these ladies carrying? Notice the elaborate dresses and tight waists. Do they look comfortable? It was the fashion in the Edwardian Age to wear very tight corsets to nip the waist and give the lady what was called the 'hour-glass look'. Why was it given this strange name?

No lady went on a weekend visit without taking her personal maid to fetch hot water for baths, look after her clothes, help her to dress and curl her hair. The maid packed her mistress's dressing-case, like the one below which is of leather with a silk lining. See if you can find these items in it:

— hair brushes, a comb and mirror
— tongs for curling the hair
— a 'stretcher' for tight gloves (in the lid, on the left)
— a button-hook, to fasten the many buttons on boots and shoes without bending
— glass jars for perfumes and creams
— the little box at the bottom right-hand corner. Girls will know what this is!

A gentleman would have a similar case but containing different things. Find out what they might be and make a labelled drawing of the case.

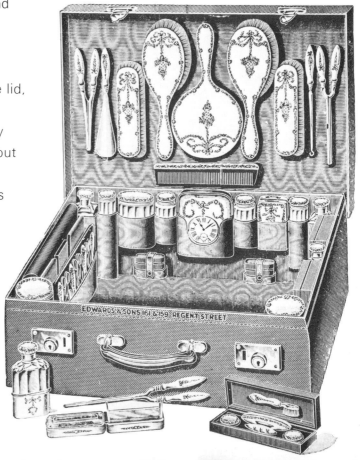

8

Weekend parties often included some shooting. Look at King Edward VII, wearing a cape, examining the 'bag' at a Sandringham shoot. Someone who knew the king said he liked 'masses of pheasants driven over his head, about the height of an ordinary tree'. Can you think why?

Cricket was played and tennis was becoming popular. In 1877 the first Wimbledon championships were held. How old would Winston Churchill have been then? Look at the figures in the advertisement below. What do the lady's long skirt and carefully-arranged hair and hat tell you about the way she played the game? Notice the oddly-shaped racquets and the cap, tight collar and bow tie worn by the two men.

### Things to do

Start a collection of work about the Edwardian Age with a section on meals. Illustrate those described in this book and compare them with the meals we eat nowadays.

Try to get a copy of *Mrs Beeton's Book of Household Management*, which has many amusing pictures and a lot of information about this period.

Imagine you have been a guest at a weekend party. Write to a friend describing the house where you stayed, the other guests and how you spent the time. Illustrate the letter to make it more interesting for your friend to read.

# The world of the poor

In the 19th century, some towns grew rapidly as people moved there, from the country, to find work. Houses were crammed into small spaces and too many people were usually squeezed into each house. A survey in one part of London found that, in certain areas, so many people were occupying some houses that some were sleeping *under* the beds while others were *in* them.

Look at this photograph taken in a part of London called Bermondsey. At the time of Winston Churchill's birth, in that great house, a large number of townspeople were living in tiny, dark houses like these. Find:
— the yard, or court, with its cobblestones. A number of houses were grouped round this.
— the lines of washing. These houses had no gardens. Would the washing get dry easily?
— the ragged-looking clothes worn by these poor children
— the door behind the children. This was the closet, or lavatory. It was shared by a number of houses.
— the standpipe, or tap, in the bottom right-hand corner. Every drop of water had to be fetched from this in buckets.

In this part of London, 25 families shared one tap and one closet. You could only get water for 2 hours a day and not at all on Sundays.

You have probably heard of Dr Barnardo. When he was trying to show people how much the poor needed help, he used this picture as a lantern-slide. It was shown on a lantern like the one on page 20. Look at the words he has scratched on the picture. From what you see, would you think they are true?

In those days people could build houses or factories almost where they wanted. Factories with smoking chimneys were built too close to houses. Some towns planned things better. Birmingham, in the 1870s, paved its streets, laid on gas and water supplies and created parks. But in 1897, at Wednesbury, a hole was left in the road for months while people argued about who should mend it.

By the end of the 19th century most towns were beginning to build streets of 'villas' like those above. Notice the LET signs in the windows, the road which is not yet made up and the gas street-lamps.

The houses on the right were thought to be luxurious and those who could afford them were envied. Look out for rows like these today in towns. There is often a slab somewhere giving the date of building.

Sometimes houses have names which give you a clue about when they were built. Try to make a collection of these names and dates. This photograph shows one called Coronation Cottages. Whose coronation was it in 1902? Check your answer on page 14.

You could buy more for your money in those days, but wages were still very low. Until 1914 most people worked 9 hours a day and 6 days a week. What are the hours now? Employers liked long hours 'to keep the workers out of mischief' they said. A dock labourer earned less than 20p a day. Some women worked at home, making things like matchboxes, or umbrellas, for 50p a week.

The family above are making brushes. You may be able to recognise some of the parts on the table. The baby has been given one to play with. Look at this poor, bare room the family lives and works in. What are the children sitting on? Notice:
— the bare floor
— the broken table-leg
— the bare feet of the two younger boys
— the eldest boy's tattered clothes.
Many children stayed away from school because they had no clothes or shoes.

A newspaper at this time described a house which had no furniture, only a few boxes. Blood marks on the walls showed where bugs and insects had been squashed. 'We've tried everything,' said the occupants, 'but as fast as we get 'em down, they come in fresh from houses on either side.'

12

In 1900 more than a million people were paupers. This means they were helpless, with no money or work, and no hope of getting any. One-third of the population did not have enough to live on properly. They ate bread and jam and filled up with suet puddings. Meat was a once-weekly treat.

Better-off families did not realise how poor some people were. When

Winston Churchill visited Manchester as a young man and saw conditions there he said, 'Fancy living in one of these streets, never seeing anything beautiful, never eating anything savoury, never saying anything clever.'

People, especially old people, who could not support themselves were usually sent to the workhouse. It might be like the one above, where dinner is in progress. Notice how many women are packed into this one room and how they are all

dressed alike, in dresses and caps. There is hardly room for their plates on those narrow tables. Yet this was one of the best workhouses. Some were terrible places. A report in the 1890s described one where the 'sick and aged, mentally deficient, lunatics, babies and children, able-bodied and tramps, were all herded together ...'.

The old woodcutter in this picture, hearing he was being sent to the workhouse, said, 'I'd sooner lie down and die by the side of the road, and I'd do it too.'

In 1908 some important laws were passed to help people. By then Winston Churchill had grown up and was a Member of Parliament. His friend and colleague, David Lloyd George, persuaded Parliament to pay people over 70 a weekly pension. This was 25p, or 35½p for a married couple. It was enough to save many from the workhouse.

How much is the old-age pension now and how old must people be to get it? Is it still called by that name?

This photograph was taken on the day the first old-age pensions were paid. Compare the way people dressed then and now. Women were considered quite old when they were only 50. They usually wore black, with shawls and bonnets like these. The older men wore beards and whiskers and it was thought strange to go without a hat.

Another law was made to pay an unemployment benefit to those who could not find work and another made it easier for poorer people to get medical help if they needed it.

The Post Office letter-box in the first picture has the king's initials, ER. Here he is, with his queen, on a souvenir biscuit-tin. Find their initials and the date of the coronation. Draw a family tree to show how Queen Elizabeth II and her children are descended from this king and queen. Find or draw pictures of the people in your 'tree' to illustrate it.

## Illness

In this photograph of a hospital ward, look carefully at all these things:
— the two nurses, in stiff starched aprons, with caps tied under the chin. Their dresses were made of thick unwashable material called serge. Only in our own century have washable clothes been introduced.
— the matron. How is her uniform different from the nurses?
— the iron or brass cots for the children
— the curious stove in the centre of the ward
— a progress report hanging over each cot. Where are these kept in a modern hospital?

This is the children's ward in Ipswich hospital, just about the time when Winston Churchill was born. Ipswich was proud of its hospital. In other towns sick people had to put up with much less attractive conditions.

The ward is light and clean, but does it seem a cheerful place for children? What can you see to keep them amused? If you have ever been in hospital, or visited someone there, compare the ward with this one. Make a list of all the differences you can think of. Make a drawing of this room, then draw or find a picture of a modern hospital ward to put with it. Write captions for your pictures.

Doctors generally wore frock coats, like the one on the left, even when performing operations. Not until about 1900 did they adopt white washable overalls, like this one. Rubber gloves were worn more to protect the surgeon's hands than to safeguard the patient.

Below you can see the kind of uniform worn by nurses in 1905.

Almost all doctors were men. But in the same year that Winston Churchill was born, the London School of Medicine for Women had been opened and by 1901 there were 335 women doctors.

Illness was one of poor people's greatest fears. Since 1948 we have had a National Health Service through which patients can get all or part of their treatment and medicine free (see page 60). But in the early days of this century being ill might mean calling the doctor and perhaps buying medicine. If all the children in a large family caught something like influenza, the doctor's bill could be as much as half a week's wages.

The figures in the chart on the next page show how many people died from certain diseases. None of these is considered a real killer now and all can be treated by modern drugs and surgery. You have probably been given injections in your childhood to prevent you catching some of these illnesses. But look how many died of measles, for example, in 1900 compared with 1960.

One reason why our health has improved so much is that we live in better conditions now and eat more nourishing food. Our bodies can fight the germs that attack them. In 1889, 50,000 children in London schools were reported to be undernourished. One inspector wrote, 'Puny, pale-faced, scantily-clad and badly shod, these small and feeble folk may be found limp and chill on the school benches in all the poorer parts of London.' Fifty years after that was written school meals and milk and the medical service had made British children stronger and healthier.

Number of deaths from certain diseases

|                 | 1900 | 1922 | 1940 | 1960 |
|-----------------|------|------|------|------|
| Measles         | 394  | 149  | 21   | 1    |
| TB              | 1902 | 1121 | 699  | 75   |
| Bronchitis      | 1692 | 1073 | 1120 | 579  |
| Pneumonia       | 1374 | 1073 | 734  | 548  |
| Whooping-cough  | 356  | 167  | 17   | 1    |
| Influenza       | 504  | 563  | 286  | 24   |
| Diphtheria      | 290  | 107  | 62   | 0    |

Use the figures in this table to draw graphs showing how diseases have become less dangerous. Use a different colour for each. Make them large enough to add drawings, showing what doctors, nurses and hospitals have looked like in the years 1900–1960. The pictures in this book will give you a start. It should be easy to find some modern ones.

Interview your parents and grandparents about being ill or in hospital when they were your age. Put their descriptions with your graphs. Use reference books to find something about X-rays (Röntgen), penicillin (Fleming) and sulphonamide drugs and how these have all helped us.

# The world of a child

Look at these two girls out with their 'nanny' or nursemaid, early this century. Would you think they are from a rich family or a poor one? Notice:

— their beautiful white fur coats and hats. Compare the hats with the one in the advertisement on page 25.

— the curious pram, with its large and small wheels

— the plain, dark clothes the nursemaid wears and the little bonnet perched on top of her head. Clothes like these, although dull-looking to us, were the correct dress for a nursemaid employed by a well-to-do family.

The children of rich families often saw very little of their parents. Their nurse might bring them down to the drawing-room just before bedtime, to be fussed and petted by their parents, or perhaps shown off to visitors.

The Churchills were busy, important people. Winston's father was an important man in the Government. Of his mother, the boy wrote, 'I loved her dearly — but at a distance.'

Winston's nurse, Nanny Everest, took charge of him when he was a year old. He said later, 'Mrs Everest it was who looked after me and tended all my wants. It was to her I poured out all my many troubles.'

Read this letter he wrote to her when he was 10. What was his pet name for her? And what did he call himself? The letter is about his bad cough. After reading it, what do you think about his spelling and handwriting?

When Winston was 7 and 'what grown-up people in their off-hand way called a troublesome boy', he was sent to a boarding school. It was fashionable and expensive, but had a cruel headmaster. He used to thrash boys who had done wrong, while the whole school listened to their screams. 'I counted the days and the hours to the end of every term when I could return home and range my soldiers in line of battle on the nursery floor,' wrote Churchill later, when he was grown up.

He had nearly 1,000 toy soldiers. His childhood friends remembered that he was always preparing them to fight against what he called 'the enemies of England'. And they recalled these games and battles many years later when, as Britain's leader, he was determined to save his country from Hitler and the Germans.

Most boys of the 'upper classes' were sent to schools called Public Schools, many of which are very famous. Winston went to Harrow when he was 13. Compare the way he is dressed in this photograph above with the school advertisement here. The top hat, stiff collar and stick were an important part of the Public School uniform. Find all 3 in both pictures.

Harrow School looked like this when Winston attended it. Compare it with your own school.

Winston was not much of a scholar. Once, on an examination paper, he wrote nothing except his name. Later he made a bargain with a friend. This boy did Winston's daily Latin exercise for him in return for help with his English essays. Later on

Winston wrote of his schooldays, 'I would far rather have been apprenticed as a bricklayer's mate or run errands as a messenger boy. It would have been more real.'

What he enjoyed most, and remembered best, were the famous people who sometimes came to Harrow to tell the boys about great battles, or mountain climbing. Later, when he became a soldier, he found he loved reading history and writing it too!

These school talks were often illustrated by slides on a magic lantern like this one. Can you see that it is really 3 lanterns, one above the other? In this way one picture could be made to merge into the next, giving a sense of movement. This was exciting, in the days before real moving pictures. The lantern was lit by a mixture of oxygen and hydrogen, which could be dangerous. Find the chimney on top where the fumes escaped.

If your parents were poor it was a different story. Until 1870 you might not have gone to school at all. But in that year Parliament passed an Education Act ordering education to be provided for all children in England and Wales. The Member of Parliament who persuaded the others that this was necessary gave them some facts and figures to make them think. In the great city of Liverpool, he said, there were 80,000 children — 40,000 of them (half) went to school, 20,000 (one quarter) never went, another 20,000 (one quarter) went to a school of some kind, but got 'an education not worth having'. What do you think he meant by those words? He said, too, that the rest of the country was just as bad.

Think of at least two reasons why many parents did not send their children to school until the law made them do so. The pictures on pages 10 and 12 should give you some ideas about this.

In the years following the Education Act many schools were built like this one in a country village. Can you see a tablet over the doorway? The photograph on the right is a close-up of this. Look at the date. Make a point of looking at all school buildings to see if they have a date on them. Perhaps there is one on your own school.

Look at the photographs on these two pages. The first one was taken in 1909. Can you see that some of the children have not kept still and are blurred on the photograph? Notice how they are all dressed. Compare these boys' collars with young Winston's on page 19.

The boys have short, cropped hair. Can you suggest why? It may help if you remember that very few homes then had bathrooms or a hot-water supply. At about this time one teacher reported that 28 of the 30 girls in his school had lice (insects) in their long hair, but almost all the boys were free of them.

Compare this classroom with your own by looking at:
— the hard wooden desks. Children sat on a seat which was part of the desk. It probably hurt their backs and made them wriggle.
— the dull walls of painted bricks. There are some framed pictures, but nothing like the cheerful display of things you probably have in your room.
— the dreary-looking plants in flowerpots on one window-sill.

Make a list of the things your classroom has to make it bright and comfortable, that this room does not have.

You would find a school like that one strange, uncomfortable and dull. Teachers were strict. Children were not allowed to move around, or talk, except when they were told to. They spent much of the school day sitting at those hard desks learning things by heart, instead of being allowed and encouraged to find out for themselves. One girl remembered spending hours reciting the alphabet. When they reached Z the children just went back to A and said it all over again.

Classes were often very large. At the school on page 21 some of the older girls were allowed to teach the youngest children so that the teacher could spend more time with her senior pupils.

This picture was taken in 1920 after the First World War. Do the children look happier than those in the last photograph? What changes can you notice in their clothes? Most boys still wore caps.

Show these pictures to your grandparents and great-grandparents and see what they say about them. Ask them to tell you about their schooldays — what they wore, how lessons were carried on, whether they had any games and whether they enjoyed school on the whole. Then use that information to write some short reports about schools in past days compared with now. Draw some children and classrooms of past times and our own times to show the differences.

Some children whose parents could afford the fees went to private schools. It used to be thought that girls did not need much education. It was enough for a girl to be able to sew and sing and play the piano. Girls sometimes learnt all sorts of odd bits of general knowledge, such as the dates of all the kings and queens, but not much else. This began to change after about 1870.

Read this advertisement for a girls' private school in 1920. Which parts of it suggest that girls at this school received a fairly thorough education?

## "LAMORNA" School for Girls,
### 41, Kirkley Cliff, LOWESTOFT.

### Miss KIDNER, Principal,
#### late of ARDMORE, NORTH PARADE.

Owing to increase of pupils the principal has removed to the larger premises at Kirkley Cliff.

French and Music Specialities.
Definite Religious Training (Ch. of Eng.).
Foreign, Resident and Visiting Mistresses.
Preparation for Higher and Local Exams.
Entire Charge taken of Colonial Children.
Individual Care of Delicate Children.
Dry Bracing Air.     House facing Sea.
Physical Culture.     Plenty of Outdoor Life.
Moderate Terms.     Lady Matron.

## Things to do

On page 21 you were told about schools and children in Liverpool before the Education Act. Draw a block graph based on those figures and give it a title.

| | |
|---|---|
| 1893 | 11 years |
| 1899 | 12 years |
| 1918 | 14 years |
| 1944 | 15 years |
| 1973 | 16 years |

This table shows how the school-leaving age has been raised over 80 years. Turn this information into a graph or a block diagram. Give it a title and add some illustrations of schools and schoolchildren over that period.

Examine your home area for school buildings with a date on them, like the one on page 21. Copy any dates and inscriptions you find and make a chart of them.

If your school is an old one it may have some pictures of school life in past years. Your relations may have similar pictures from their own schooldays. If you can borrow these and write captions for them you can arrange your own exhibition about schools and education in the age of Winston Churchill.

# Entertainment

When there was not so much ready-made entertainment at home, such as television, both children and adults made the most of everything there was.

The coming of railways, horse-buses and motor vehicles made it possible to spend a day by the sea, or at a local beauty-spot. That is where these children are off to. It is August 1914, only a day or two before the First World War began. This is their annual school treat, which is why they are all wearing their best clothes. Look at the girls' big hats. Compare them with the one below which is from a shop catalogue of the same year, 1914. How can you tell, from the horses, that this was a special occasion?

One boy whose mother used to arrange village outings remembered all the preparations, especially how everyone saved their money all the year for the big day.

He remembered how smart everyone looked when they set off and how grubby when they came home — just like nowadays! There was always a fuss about who should sit where. All the boys wanted to sit next to the driver, hoping he might let them take the reins.

The horses were rested and fed every 20 kilometres. Their nosebags and water-buckets were slung underneath the wagon. To help the horses when they reached a hill, everyone got out, walked up the hill and climbed in again at the top.

The children in both pictures here are enjoying themselves at the seaside in much the same way that children do now. Notice:
- the children's clothes. How do they compare with the way that *you* dress at the seaside? Which items of clothing seem especially unsuitable for the beach?
- the girl in the first picture with her frilly dress and big, floppy hat. This was in case the sunshine might be too strong for her!
- her tightly-buttoned boots. They hardly seem sensible for playing on the sand. Can you remember how all those little buttons were fastened? (See page 8.)
- the puppet show, Punch and Judy. It was a favourite on the beach. Have you ever watched a Punch and Judy show, or seen one on television, or in a book?
- the boy wearing a sailor's collar. Sailor suits, in those days, were a popular kind of 'best clothes' for both boys and girls.

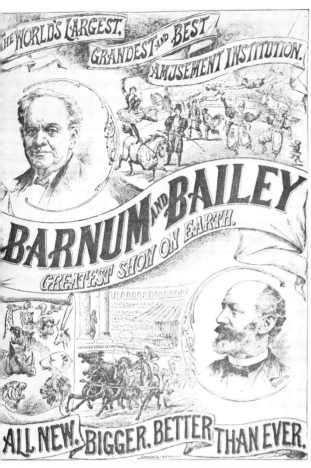

If the weather was bad there were some indoor amusements, but fewer than nowadays.

The circus was always popular. Look at this programme-cover of an American circus visiting Britain in 1898. Read what it claims to be. The pictures on the programme were to give you an idea of some of the circus acts. From looking at them, do you think circuses have changed much since this time?

The first moving-picture show in Britain was in 1896. People called it 'the flicks' because of its strange jerky movements. By 1920 there were 4,000 cinemas. Some were not very clean and many parents would not allow their children to visit them.

Then in 1928 came talking pictures. This photograph shows an early film being made with very simple equipment. Look for:
— the actor, or 'film star', holding a gun
— the microphone hanging above him
— the director on a stool, checking the actor's words from a copy of the play
— the producer, wearing earphones, checking the sound-track

Mickey Mouse was first seen that same year in a film called *Steamboat Willie*.

In the year Winston Churchill was born, 1874, Aston Villa became the first football club to charge admission to matches. More and more people spent Saturday afternoons watching players like this taking part in the popular game. Photographers were not able to take 'action' shots. Their cameras and films were not good enough. This photograph was taken in a studio against a painted background. The striped shirt has not changed much, but look at those 'shorts'!

The biggest crowd that had ever watched a football match — 110,820 people — saw the 1901 Cup Final at the Crystal Palace. Then the new Wembley Stadium was

built and the 1923 Cup Final was played there. 125,000 spectators saw Bolton Wanderers beat West Ham 2–0 and 35,000 more people broke into the ground and ran on to the pitch. Look at the policemen edging them back.

Wembley Stadium has become our most famous sports arena.

## Things to do

Draw the wagon from page 25 and draw a modern motor coach to put beside it. Write a heading and a caption for both pictures.

Make a list of things you find at the seaside now, but can't see in the pictures on page 26.

Find which sporting events are held at Wembley Stadium each year.

Try to find what nickname was given to the first talking pictures. Ask older relatives the names of some of the early 'stars' they remember and see if they have any picture postcards of them.

# The First World War (1914–18)

When he left school, young Winston Churchill became an army officer-cadet at Sandhurst. This was the life he liked. 'We dug trenches ... and learned how to blow up masonry bridges.' He passed his course easily. 'I could learn quickly enough the things that mattered,' he wrote.

He served with the army in India. Then, in 1899, he went to South Africa as a news reporter to cover a war in South Africa (the Boer War). It provided plenty of adventure, for he was captured and escaped. This poster offered a reward for him, dead or alive. Find his name and the amount of the reward. Nobody got it though, because he stowed away in a goods-train and reached safety. Back home again, he became a Member of Parliament.

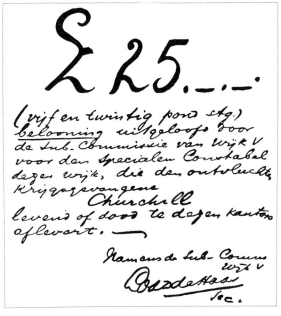

Here are King George V and Queen Mary in their splendid coronation robes. Look at their crowns and the queen's jewels. They were the grandparents of Queen Elizabeth II. Find out when their reign began.

In 1914 Churchill was First Lord of the Admiralty. King George wrote in his diary one day, 'Winston Churchill came to see me. The Navy is all ready for war, but please God it will not come.' The Prime Minister joked that 'Winston, who has got on all his war paint, is longing for a sea fight.'

The First World War began on 4th August 1914.

There were many reasons for this war, the 'Great War' as people called it. Britain went to war because Germany attacked Belgium which we had promised to protect.

Europe had had no big war for nearly 50 years. Young men thought it would be an adventure. They rushed to join the army before 'the fun' was over. Most people expected we would beat the Germans by Christmas.

   Posters like this appeared everywhere, encouraging men to enlist. Do you know the great admiral who, in a different war, first used that sentence about expecting every man to do his duty?

Look at these men being medically examined for the army and look for:
— another recruiting poster on the wall
— the men being examined. Does the one on the right look old enough to be a soldier?
— the doctors in their strange, formal clothes. Look back at page 16 to remind yourself how doctors still dressed.
— the two men sitting at the table. What are they doing?

In 1917 only 36 men out of every 100 examined were perfectly fit. What does this tell you about the conditions in which most people lived at this time?

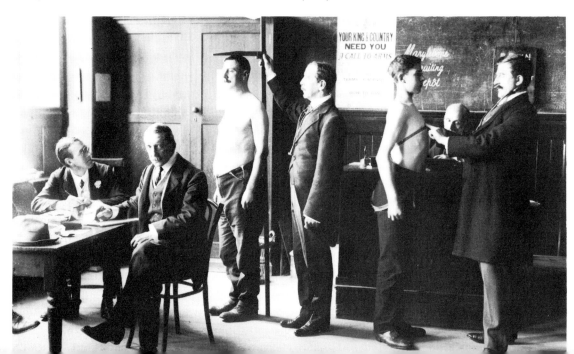

## The war on land

A few days after war was declared 80,000 men of the BEF (British Expeditionary Force) crossed the Channel to join the fighting in France.

At this stage of the war supplies and guns were usually hauled by horses. Later, passenger buses were converted for use as troop transports. The two in this picture came from London. Look for:

- their boarded-up windows
- a spade and pick-axe fixed to one bus. What might these be used for?
- the pile of equipment on top of one bus
- the amount of personal equipment carried by the soldiers. Each man wore and carried a total of 65 lbs (29 kg).

In France, where the fighting took place, the two sides faced each other from their trenches. The area in between was called 'no-man's land'. One soldier remembered it as 'a horrible churned-up place, all pock-marked with shell-holes, and covered with barbed wire and old gun-carriages'.

Winston Churchill spent a good deal of time at the fighting area. One day his dug-out was blown up by a shell 5 minutes after he left it. A general remarked that this was 'a very dangerous place'. Churchill is supposed to have replied, 'Yes, sir, but, after all, this is a very dangerous war!'

Sometimes the British and French attacked, rushing from their trenches with bayonets fixed to their rifles. This was called going 'over the top'. They charged across 'no-man's land' to capture the first line of enemy trenches and push the Germans back to their second line. Next time it might be the Germans who made the attack, pushing the British back. Terrible battles and heavy casualties sometimes gained or lost only a few metres of ground.

These soldiers, the Lancashire Fusiliers, are waiting to go 'over the top'. Here are some things to look for which can tell you a lot about trench warfare:
—sandbags to give protection from bullets and shell-fire
—the trench walls of earth. In winter rain and frost filled the trenches with mud. The men might have to wade through the mud up to their knees.
—signs. The trench network was complicated so soldiers put up these signs to help them find their way. There are 3 more on this page.
—some men are fixing bayonets to their rifles and others have already done so
—notice how all vegetation has been blasted off the landscape. In some parts of France and Belgium it has never grown properly again since these battles.

This was the Battle of the Somme, in France, in 1916. On the first day of that battle 20,000 men were killed or died from their wounds.

It is hard for us to imagine how unpleasant life in the trenches was. In winter many men suffered from frostbite — fingers or toes dropped off. The food was almost always poor and cooking it was a problem.

Look at this soldier preparing a meal and pick out:
— the 'stove' he is using. It is an old tin, punched with holes, filled with fire and used as a brazier.

— those round tins with handles. They are called mess tins and they were part of a soldier's equipment. Food was cooked in them and eaten from them.
— the soldier's cap, with two flaps fastened on top. These could be lowered to cover the ears. What for? If you can't think, read the first part of this page again.

Hard biscuits, sometimes given out instead of bread, needed soaking before they could be eaten. One soldier joked, 'When we tried the biscuits we knew why the men with bad teeth had been turned down at the medical inspection.' Another said the war taught him a lesson. 'Never through the remainder of my life have I grumbled at a poor meal.'

In 1915 the Germans used a new weapon — poison gas. By 1916 soldiers were being issued with helmets like these, clumsy and uncomfortable. Look at the two eyepieces and the nose-flap which allowed you to breathe. Helmets like this gave little protection against the fumes. Later ones were more satisfactory.

The war produced some strange new vehicles. Look at this armoured car with a machine-gun sticking out at the front.

In 1917, at the battle of Cambrai, the first tanks were used successfully.

Winston Churchill had shown interest in developing the tank as a weapon. The War Minister, Lord Kitchener, had thought it useless, and called it 'a pretty mechanical toy'.

The first ones were described as 'water tanks' to keep their real purpose secret from the enemy. They could cross ditches, crush barbed wire and capture as much ground in a day as had previously taken 3 months.

Tanks sometimes broke down on rough ground. Read this description by a young soldier and then compare it with this photograph of a stranded tank. Identify all the parts he mentions.

'... My first impression was that they looked ready to topple over on their noses, but their tails and the two little wheels at the back held them down.... Big metal things they were, with two sets of caterpillar wheels that went right round the body. There was a bulge on each side, with a door in the bulging part and machine-guns on swivels poked out from either side.'

That description does not mention the curious wood and wire frame on top. Can you think what this might have been for?

# The war in the air

When war began there were only 2,000 airmen. Some were in the Royal Naval Air Service, others in the Royal Flying Corps. Both of these were formed in 1912. The RFC badge was worn on the shoulders of the airmen. How is this uniform different from that of a modern airman? In April 1918 the RNAS and RFC were joined and became the Royal Air Force.

Aircraft like those in the picture were useful in war. They could fly over the enemy's trenches and observe troop movements. Later in the war they were fitted with push-button machine-guns to attack enemy planes. Notice the two seats — one for the pilot and one for a passenger.

The Germans built great airships called Zeppelins. They were built round an aluminium framework, covered with a waterproof skin and filled with hydrogen. Some were as much as 200 metres long. The control cars were slung underneath. You can just see them in the picture of a Zeppelin in flames on the next page. They were hard to destroy because they could climb much higher than the little aircraft. One pilot said that looking for a Zeppelin at night was 'like trying to find a fly in a dark room'.

Why was aluminium, rather than steel, used for the Zeppelin's framework?

The damage here was done in an air raid. A Zeppelin bomb hit the house on the left. Two soldiers came home on leave a few days later. They found their home in ruins and their mother dead.

Look for the troops guarding the site and the wreckage all over the road. For the first time ordinary people were now being attacked and involved in the horrors of war. During the First World War 1,414 people were killed and 3,416 injured in air raids on Britain.

Occasionally a Zeppelin was shot down. Read the caption to this souvenir picture. Look how the plane has been turned upside down. Unfortunately, 2 weeks after he had destroyed this Zeppelin, the pilot of this plane was killed in action. Can you see how 2 extra lines of printing have been stuck on to bring the story up to date?

THE V.C "ZEP" WRECKER.
Flight Sub-Lieutenant R.A.J. Warneford, who destroyed a Zeppelin with bombs at a height of 6,000 Ft. The Explosion caused his machine to turn upside down, but he righted himself and landed in enemy country, escaped, but was killed a fortnight later while testing a new Aeroplane near Paris.

## The war at home

When war came the Government took precautions to keep Britain and her people safe.

The coasts were guarded, especially after German battleships bombarded Scarborough, Whitby and Hartlepool on the east coast. 127 people were killed.

Observation posts were set up. This one, called a 'pill-box' because of its shape, is in East Anglia. Look at the iron doors and the small window through which an approaching enemy could be shot.

Despatch-riders on motor cycles kept army posts in touch with each other. This man has a warm coat. His goggles are pushed up. Why would he need to wear them? One civilian said, 'They rush through the village at speeds estimated up to 50 mph [80 km/h].'

At sea, German submarines attacked merchant ships bringing us food. In the spring of 1917 they sank more than 600. Food in Britain became scarce. 4,000 people queued one day outside a butcher's shop. Then, in January 1918, certain foods were rationed. This meant that everybody was allowed to buy the same small amount and no-one had to go without.

## Armistice Day

In 1918, at the 11th hour of the 11th day of the 11th month the war ended. The German leaders asked for an armistice. A German corporal heard the news and said that it was 'terrible to bear'. His name was Adolf Hitler.

Everyone wanted to punish Germany and make her pay the cost of the war. Winston Churchill thought this was a mistake. If Germany was treated too harshly, he said, she would bear a grudge for ever and would always be looking for ways of getting revenge on her conquerors. This was just what did happen and Churchill saw that a chance of bringing lasting peace to Europe had been lost.

Look at this scene in Westminster Abbey. In 1920 the body of one unknown soldier was brought from France and buried there. Pick out:
- the coffin, covered with a Union Jack
- 4 servicemen standing guard
- people filing past the grave. In the few days following the ceremony, more than a million people came to see the tomb at the west end of the abbey, just inside the door.

This was Britain's way of remembering and honouring all those who had died for their country.

## Things to do

The 1914–18 war can make an exciting exhibition. Here are some ideas.

Every village and town has a war memorial, often in the church or churchyard. Look at as many as you can. Try to find the population of the place in 1914, then count how many died in the war.

Some of these memorials have interesting (and sometimes gruesome) pictures, statues and wording. You may be able to sketch them, or take photographs of them, for your exhibition.

Use reference books to find all you can about the following men. Then write a short account of each, with a picture or drawing. Make your work into a chart or a zig-zag album.
King George V
the Kaiser (the German Emperor)
Count Zeppelin (inventor of the airship)
Lord Kitchener (Secretary for War)
David Lloyd George (Prime Minister)
Winston Churchill's work during the war
the Unknown Warrior

Make models of a Zeppelin, a tank, an armoured car, a pill-box, a gas-mask and some of the trench signs.

Draw a large map of Belgium and north-east France. Then use a good historical atlas or reference books to find the places where battles were fought in this war. Mark their names on the map.

Many families have photographs of soldiers, or letters and postcards sent home by soldiers from the battlefields. See if you can borrow some of these and write explanations to go with them.

Find out how the armistice was celebrated in your own village or town. The newspapers of November 1918 (in your town library) should have a lot about this, perhaps including some pictures.

Visit, if you can, the Imperial War Museum in London. The story of the war is vividly told there and books, cards and posters are on sale.

*Goodbye to all that*, by Robert Graves, has exciting descriptions of life (and death) in the trenches. You would probably enjoy reading parts of this book.

# Life between the wars

The men standing in this queue are waiting outside an Employment Exchange, a place where people go to see what jobs are available. The year is 1924 and they are all out of work. Look at their shabby clothes. Find the man coming out with something in his hand. This is his dole, a small sum of money paid weekly by the Government to people without jobs.

The soldiers and sailors who fought in the war had been promised 'a land fit for heroes to live in'. But when they came home, expecting to find it, many found they had no work to return to. When the war ended many factories and shipyards closed down. There was no more need for tanks, guns or ships. By 1921 more than 2 million people were unemployed.

One man worked only 11 days in 8 years. A woman whose husband was out of work for 12 years told a reporter she had just patched a shirt for the 8th time. Her husband did all the family's shoe repairs and hair cutting, patched the kettle and soldered handles on to old tins to make mugs. They had no money for newspapers, holidays or entertainments.

Men who are out of work for a long time feel ashamed that they cannot earn money to support their families. A Glasgow man remembered 'street corners where men were standing around, wondering whatever dead-end job they could pick up'. What do you think is meant by 'dead-end'?

Look at this man standing on a street corner and notice:
— his shabby clothes. Both trouser-legs are patched.
— his shoes. They are clogs with wooden soles to last as long as possible.
— the way he hangs his head. Why is he doing this?

Because of these conditions, 635,000 people left Britain between 1921 and 1925 and went to live in other countries.

In 1926 there was a General Strike, started by miners wanting better conditions. Workers in many important industries supported them. While this short, grim strike was on, the Government published its own newspaper, which Winston Churchill edited. Here is a part of the first page. Churchill made the strikers angry. A born fighter himself, he looked on them as 'the enemy' and called the strike 'a challenge to Parliament'.

The General Strike lasted only 9 days. But the miners stayed out until winter. Then they were forced to return to work and had to put up with lower wages and longer working hours.

In spite of the unemployment and hardships, living conditions for most people improved between the two world wars.

Better houses were built on the edges of London and other big towns. More people were able to have electricity in their homes now. Visitors to the 1920 Ideal Home Exhibition saw an 'all-electric' house, with fires, kettle, toaster, iron and water-heater. Look at these 2 electric cookers. One was made in the 1930s and the other is a modern one. What are the differences between them?

The Broadcasting Service began in 1922. By the following year concerts, weather forecasts and Big Ben's chimes were all regular features on the radio. School broadcasts started in 1924 and racing, cricket and tennis in 1927. A wireless, or radio, licence cost 50p a year. Do you still need a licence if you own a radio now?

Here is King George V, at Christmas 1932, making the first royal broadcast to his people. Look at the 2 strange microphones on the table.

The BBC began a television service in 1936. It stopped 3 years later when war broke out and did not develop further until the late 1940s.

Design a time-chart called 'Broadcasting, 1922–39'. Draw pictures to illustrate all the different kinds of programmes and when they began, such as 1924 – broadcasts to schools. Add titles and short descriptions.

## Progress in the air

The *Daily Mail* newspaper offered £10,000 to the first man to fly an aeroplane across the Atlantic Ocean. In 1919 Alcock and Whitten-Brown set out to win this prize. Their old Vickers-Vimy war plane had its bomb racks removed to make extra space for 3,932 litres of fuel. The 2 men sat in the open cockpit with no radio or any of the modern aids to navigation. Ice formed on the wings and sleet obscured their view, but they succeeded and crash-landed in Ireland as this photograph shows. Notice how clumsy the plane seems with its 2 sets of wings and wire supports, and the long body. You can see it in London's Science Museum.

Winston Churchill, who was then Secretary for Air, compared their journey to that of Christopher Columbus. He said they could have been doomed by 'a drop of water in the carburettor or a spot of oil in their plugs'.


Alcock and Brown took just over 16 hours to fly 3,024 km. Work out their average speed from this. How long do planes take to cross the Atlantic now? What do they have to help them navigate?

Turn back to pages 35 and 36 and remind yourself about the Zeppelin airships. The British Government were interested in airships too. Winston Churchill thought they would be no use in war, but could be useful for carrying large numbers of passengers.

Several huge airships were built. The *R34* was as big as an ocean liner and could cruise smoothly at 60 mph (96 km/h). Look at the *R101* at its mooring-mast. The buildings give you an idea of its size. It held 100 passengers. But a terrible disaster happened. A few hours after taking off for India, it crashed. The wreckage in the picture below was all that was left. 48 people lost their lives. One survivor said, 'It was just one mass of flame roaring like a furnace.'

After this Britain built no more airships, but other men and women continued to make longer and more successful flights in aeroplanes. Here are some names to look up to find what each did:
Ross and Keith Smith
Charles Lindbergh
Charles Kingsford-Smith
Amy Johnson
Jim Mollison
Amelia Earhart

Use books in your library to make a picture-chart about aeroplanes and airships in the years 1919–39.

## The motor car age

In 1896 the first-ever Motor Show was held in London. That same year a woman was knocked down by a car and killed. This was the first fatal motoring accident.

People were at first suspicious of this new form of transport. But London's last horse-buses ran in 1911 and in the following year the people in this photograph

went on their works outing in a new kind of bus, called a charabanc. It could travel at nearly 20 mph (32 km/h). Its name was French, meaning 'a carriage with benches'. Does this seem a good name for it? How many passengers will this one hold? What do you think the strange object fixed on to the back is?

Look for the petrol tanks on the two motor cycles here. Where is the engine and how do you suppose it drives the machine? Can you see the horns, and the number plates? After 1903 all vehicles had by law to be registered and given numbers.

Motor cycles, then as now, were especially popular with young men. When the First World War ended in 1918, many ex-soldiers bought them with their gratuities, the money they received when they left the army. The machines often had to be started up by what was called the 'run-alongside-and-jump-on' method.

Motor cars, in their early days, were troublesome too. The wife of one car owner kept a diary. Here are 3 of the entries for one year:

'Nov. 24    Played with our motor—no result.

Dec. 9    Awful crowd followed us at Cosham; had to beat them off with umbrella.

Dec. 27    Frightened an unattended horse attached to a milk cart, which bolted and sent the milk cans flying in all directions.'

Boys used to hang around in villages, hoping to earn some pocket-money by helping to push a broken-down motor car to the nearest garage.

Look at this garage of about 1926 and find:
— the car inside being repaired
— the hand-operated petrol pump. The first of these was set up by the AA in 1920. Before that motorists had to carry their petrol with them in cans.
— the advertisements for petrol, oil and motor parts. How many can you find which are still on sale nowadays?

|              | 1918   | 1920    | 1930      | 1939      |
|--------------|--------|---------|-----------|-----------|
| **Motor cars** | 77,707 | 186,801 | 1,056,214 | 2,034,400 |
| **Motor cycles** | 69,206 | 287,739 | 724,315 | 418,000 |

These figures show how many cars and motor cycles were on the roads between the end of the First World War and the start of the Second World War. Draw a simple graph for each set of figures. Then try to decide:

(a) Why did the number of motor cycles increase so much between 1918 and 1920? (See page 46.)

(b) Why should the number of motor cycles have gone down by 1939?

(c) Between 1930 and 1939 the number of cars almost doubled. From this fact, what can you suggest about the price of cars and the way they were made?

In reference books, look up the names of William Morris (Lord Nuffield), Henry Ford and Herbert Austin. Write a section about each of them, saying what he did for motoring.

Try to find, or draw, pictures of all forms of transport from 1900 to the present day. Arrange them as a frieze in order of their ages. Put the name and date of each model and think of a title for the whole frieze. It is a good idea to do this on a roll of paper, such as wallpaper, so that you can extend your frieze for as long as you need.

## The League of Nations

An important meeting is in progress. It is 1926, the place is Geneva in Switzerland and this is the first conference of the League of Nations. Find the President standing up in his box in the centre to address the meeting.

The other men are representatives of many of the world's countries, because the League was hoping to prevent future wars. Countries who quarrelled with each other would bring their quarrel to the League and try to settle it there instead of fighting about it. If one country attacked another, the rest would force that country to stop and refuse to trade with her.

This seems a good idea, but an organisation like this only works well if all its members obey the rules. The United States of America would not join. Some other countries were selfish. They only supported the League when it decided to do things that they agreed with.

The League of Nations did good work in other ways. It helped to control the sale and use of drugs and it helped to improve conditions of work and health in some of the world's backward countries.

Do you remember (page 38) how a German called Hitler heard about his country's defeat in 1918? Here he is, 20 years later, on the right of this photograph. He was now the ruthless leader of Germany. Backed by his Nazi party, he meant to make his country the greatest power in Europe.

The swastika, that strange cross on Hitler's armband, was the Nazi party's badge. The Nazis got rid of people who spoke out against things they did. One night, called 'the night of the long knives', hundreds were rounded up and murdered. Winston Churchill, who could see what Hitler was aiming at, said, 'This massacre showed that conditions in Germany bore no resemblance to those of a civilised state.' But a great many people took a different view. Some insisted that Hitler was doing good and useful work in Germany. They were afraid of starting another terrible war. So they accused Churchill of being a 'warmonger' and making a fuss about nothing.

Look at the other man in the photograph. This is the Italian leader, Mussolini. His followers were called Fascists. Hitler is wearing their badge — a bundle of rods — on his arm too, above the swastika.

Hitler and Mussolini were dictators. This means that they ruled as they pleased, without having to be elected by a majority of their people.

## The return of world war

In 1935 Italy attacked Abyssinia. Then Germany invaded Austria in 1938. Everyone hoped the League of Nations would stop them, but the League had not enough support, nor an army of its own. When the dictators got away with such easy victories, they were eager for more.

The British Prime Minister, Neville Chamberlain, thought he understood Hitler and could deal with him. He flew to Germany in September 1938 to talk to Hitler. Look at the above photograph of him on his return, holding a news conference at the airport, and pick out:

— the aeroplane which brought him back, in the background
— the police keeping the crowd back
— the microphones set up in the centre by reporters
— the paper Chamberlain is waving. This was Hitler's promise not to go to war with Britain.

Chamberlain said this paper meant 'peace for our time' but Churchill knew it did not. 'It was demanded at the pistol's point,' he said. What did he mean? He urged that Britain should increase her army and build more planes in case war came.

If you had been in London on 3rd September 1939 you would have heard newspaper-sellers like this one, shouting the bad news. Hitler had attacked first Czechoslovakia and then Poland, so Britain and France declared war on her. India, Australia, New Zealand, Canada and South Africa all followed Britain's lead.

Draw or trace a map of Europe. Mark Germany and draw arrows to show the 3 countries Hitler invaded in 1938–39.

# The Second World War (1939–45)

When war began on 3rd September everyone expected the Luftwaffe (the German Air Force) to drop bombs on England at once, killing and injuring many people.

Look at these children at a railway station. They are being evacuated, or sent to the country for safety, travelling in groups from their schools. Pick out:
— the adults with them. Some were their teachers.
— labels tied to the children. Each label gave the child's name, address, age and other important information.
— the cases and bags carried by the children. They held a change of clothes and food for the journey.
— the square-shaped boxes the children and adults are carrying. Each box contained a gas-mask. You were told to carry it wherever you went.

Look at the children's faces. Many had never been away from home before. How do you think they felt about it? 400 boys from one school were evacuated to Blenheim Palace where Winston Churchill had been born.

Here are some more war preparations. Try to decide the reasons for them:
— after dark no lights must be shown. Windows were covered with thick curtains.
— paper strips were pasted on to windows in criss-cross patterns
— trenches were dug in parks and on recreation grounds
— London Zoo destroyed its poisonous snakes and spiders.

In spite of all this very little happened
for 6 months. People began to joke
about this 'phoney war'. Winston
Churchill called it a 'twilight war'.
What did he mean? Mr Chamberlain
said, 'Hitler has missed the bus.'

Then in May 1940 the Germans
attacked. Look at this map and
answer these questions:
—which 2 countries were invaded in
  April?
—when were Belgium and Holland
  attacked?
—when did Germany invade France?

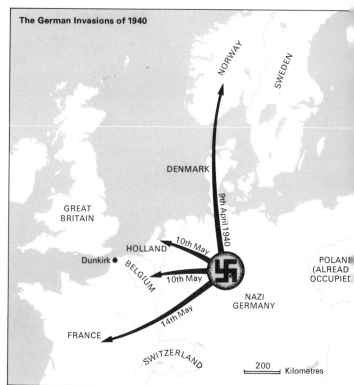

The German Invasions of 1940

When these events happened Mr
Chamberlain resigned. Parliament
decided that Churchill would be the
best leader at a time like this. On 10th
May he became Prime Minister and
Minister of Defence. He wrote in his diary
that night, 'At last I had authority to give
directions over the whole scene. I felt as
if ... all my past life had been but a
preparation for this hour and for this trial.'

This newspaper cartoon — 'Two-Gun
Winston' — shows him doing the 2 jobs.
Look at the names on the guns and the
determined look on his face. Do you
remember (page 19) how as a boy he
prepared his toy soldiers to fight 'the
enemies of England'? Now he was going
to fight a real enemy and he knew it would
be a hard fight. In his first broadcast to
the people he said, 'I have nothing to offer
but blood, toil, tears and sweat.'

52

A British army had been sent to France when war began. As the Germans pressed ahead it looked as if these soldiers would be captured. But the Royal Navy organised 'Operation Dynamo'. 800 small boats crossed the Channel to Dunkirk. (Find Dunkirk on the map on page 52.) In 9 days they rescued 338,226 men. Look at some of them

crowded on to this little steamer. Its captain said there was hardly an inch of space left on deck. Look for the French soldier in the crowd. (He is wearing a round, peaked hat.)

Soon after this France surrendered without much of a fight. Italy joined the war on Hitler's side. Mussolini felt sure Germany would win and wanted to make sure of sharing the glory.

Churchill knew that Hitler might attack Britain as he had done the other European countries. To President Roosevelt of the USA he wrote, 'We expect to be attacked ... and we are getting ready for them.'

Have you ever seen great steel masts like these? They are 115 metres tall. They could detect enemy aeroplanes coming towards them when they were still far away. With this warning our planes could get up into the sky ready to attack the Germans when they arrived overhead.

This warning-system was called radar. Its inventor, Sir Robert Watson-Watt, called it 'seeing without eyes'. Is this a good description of it? Germany had radar too, but she had not made such good progress in using it.

## The Battle of Britain and the Blitz

The Battle of Britain is the name given to the Luftwaffe's attacks throughout the summer and autumn of 1940. For 8 weeks an average of 200 enemy planes bombed London every night. There were daylight raids too, especially on the docks.

This is an Operations ('Ops') Room where information from the radar masts was collected. Look for:
- the girls with headphones and rods. They traced the course of enemy aircraft. As the planes came nearer the girls moved the symbols on the table.
- the RAF officers in the rooms above, watching the table. Through their telephones they sent instructions to planes, anti-aircraft guns and searchlights.

When the order to 'scramble' was given, pilots raced to their machines which were always standing ready. They were in the sky in a few minutes, ready to meet the German planes as they arrived.

Compare this photograph of a 'scramble' with the picture on page 35. What differences can you see between the men and the planes of the 2 world wars?

Mr and Mrs Churchill visited one of the 'ops' rooms on a day when all available planes were up fighting. There were no more reserves to call on. It was a terribly anxious moment. Later Winston praised these young pilots who fought so bravely. 'Never in the field of human conflict,' he said, 'was so much owed by so many to so few.' Who did he mean by 'the many' and 'the few'?

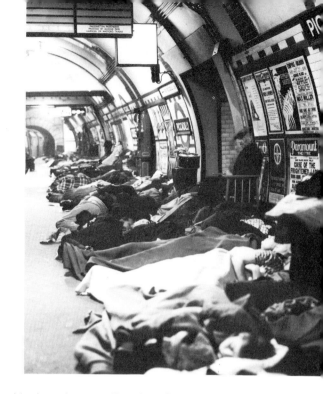

These people are sleeping in one of London's underground railway stations to be safer from the bombs. 100,000 people sheltered in these stations each night for months and months. Look how closely they are packed together. They brought rugs and blankets with them. Notice the small strip of platform left clear for people who were still travelling on the trains.

Coventry, Liverpool, Hull, Plymouth and other big cities and ports were all badly bombed. 43,000 civilians were killed in air raids during the war.

Look at Winston Churchill inspecting bomb damage. When he was touring a very poor area a crowd collected round him. They showed him the ruined houses and the

gaping bomb craters. He was moved to tears by their misfortunes and this terrible damage to their homes. Suddenly he heard a woman's surprised voice saying, 'You see, he really cares. He's crying.'

The war went on until 1945. Germany and Italy were joined by Japan. They attacked Russia and America, so both these great countries came to fight on our side.

# 'D Day' (6th June 1944)

Read this letter written to Churchill by General Montgomery. Notice the date and the reference to crossing to France. British and American troops were going to invade France, push the Germans back into Germany and end the war that way. Read the letter again. Does it sound as if Churchill and 'Monty' got on well together?

Churchill wrote in his diary that southern England was like 'a vast military camp' full of soldiers preparing for this invasion. Nearly 5,000 ships carried them and their equipment across the Channel to Normandy. This is the scene on one of the 5 invasion landing-beaches. Pick out:

— American ships (labelled US) unloading men. Notice the 'doors' which open to let the soldiers disembark, or get out.

— vehicles which have already been unloaded, standing on the beach

— big balloons flying over the beach. They were to discourage enemy planes flying low to attack.

HEADQUARTERS:
21 ARMY GROUP.
6 - 6 - 44

My dear Prime Minister

I cross over to France tonight and may not see you again for a bit. Before going I would like to thank you for many kindnesses received, and for much help and inspiration. The past 5 months have not been an easy time — for any of us. But I have always felt that you would see that all was well, and that your firm support was available at all times.

Thank you very much.

Yrs. sincerely

B. L. Montgomery

The great invasion of Normandy was successful. On 7th May 1945, 11 months later, Germany surrendered. Italy had already collapsed, so the struggle for Europe was over. Look at Churchill, in Berlin, after the war ended. He is leaving the underground shelter where Hitler killed himself rather than face defeat. About the German people, Churchill wrote, 'My hate had died with their surrender and I was much moved by their haggard looks and threadbare clothes.'

The war against Japan continued. But soon, on 6th August, the people of Hiroshima, an important Japanese harbour, saw an American plane overhead. It dropped the bomb you see below, nicknamed 'Little Boy' — the world's first atomic bomb. It was 3 times as powerful as all the explosives dropped on London in the whole of the Blitz! More than 70,000 people were killed by this one bomb. Hiroshima almost disappeared. An American who saw it soon afterwards said, 'That experience, looking down and finding nothing left of Hiroshima, was so shocking that I simply can't express what I felt.'

A few days later a second bomb was dropped on Nagasaki with similar results. Japan surrendered. The Atomic Age had begun. The Second World War was over, a war in which the whole British people were determined to defeat Hitler and all he stood for. Churchill had led them in their fight, expressed their mood in his famous speeches and planned their victory.

At the end of the war parties and celebrations went on for days. Here is Churchill going to the Houses of Parliament on Victory Day. Look at the people waving and the policemen helping to control the enormous crowd. You can scarcely see the motor car. Churchill stood up in it to speak. 'In all our long history we have never seen a greater day than this,' he said. Those near him saw tears running down his cheeks. He knew that the war had cost Britain so many men and so much money that she could never again be a leading world power.

## Things to do

Ask people you know who lived in wartime what they remember most about it. Prepare a list of things to question them about. It could include (a) evacuation, (b) air raids, (c) the black-out, (d) rationing, (e) helping the 'war effort' by collecting such things as waste paper or scrap metal. Write down your results, or interview your subjects on tape and then compile a programme about the war.

The BBC has produced a record called *Scrapbook for 1940*. If your school can buy or borrow this, it will give you some good ideas for the project above. It will also let you hear some of Churchill's most famous wartime speeches.

Many people, especially children, collected war souvenirs. Try to borrow an assortment of these for a classroom exhibition. Some possible items would be military badges, old ration books, wartime newspapers, gas-masks, letters from men and women serving in the armed forces.

Make a weapons frieze about the guns, tanks and planes used by both sides in the war.

Make your own picture gallery of famous people of the war. Get, or draw, a picture of each, and find as much information as possible to put with it. Hitler, Mussolini, Chamberlain and Montgomery are some ideas to start with. Your teacher will suggest others and how best to group them.

# The post-war years

In July 1945 there was a General Election in Britain. It was expected that Winston Churchill, who had led a united country through the war, would win. Look at him here, making an election speech. His election posters carried the words 'Help him finish the job'. What was the job?

Below is how one cartoonist in a newspaper saw the situation. The long and terrible war had exhausted everyone. In Britain, factories and ports had been destroyed by bombs; ships had been sunk; machinery had been worn out. There was a shortage of all kinds of raw materials. Soldiers would soon be home from the war and nearly 5 million houses needed building or rebuilding for them to live in.

AND NOW TO WORK

When the votes were counted it was found that the Labour Party had won, not Churchill's Conservatives. Many of the voters were young. No one wanted a return to the conditions of pre-war days. A woman who asked a soldier why he voted Labour got the answer, 'Well, Miss, anything for a change.' So Churchill, no longer Prime Minister, turned his attention to writing his history of the war and his hobbies, including painting and brick-laying.

The new Labour Government wanted to show everybody it knew how to tackle our many problems. Some of its most important and lasting work was to set up, in 1948, what is called the Welfare State. Acts of Parliament made every worker pay a certain sum of money each week. The Government added money from the taxes to this. Then nobody had to pay for treatment from doctors, dentists or opticians.

Some more advantages of the Welfare State were these:
— people out of work received money to help them live comfortably until they found jobs. Look at pages 40 and 41 again to remind yourself what happened after the First World War.
— people who were ill and could not work also received money
— widows and retired people were paid pensions
— the services of home nurses, health visitors and midwives were provided for those needing them
— clinics, like the mobile one below, were set up for mothers to get help and advice about their children and have them immunised to prevent certain diseases
— 'family allowances' were paid to help parents with the cost of bringing up their children.

Since then, as costs have increased, people have had to pay part of the cost of treatment and medicines. But anyone who is really poor can get extra help towards this and nobody who needs medical care has to go without it. The Welfare State has done a great deal of good for a great many people. But can you see any possible disadvantages in the things it does? You will need to think hard about this.

Make a chart about the Welfare State. Find out how much working people pay now in weekly contributions and put this in the centre. Then get pictures to illustrate all the services provided — doctors, clinics and so on. Arrange these round your chart. Write headings and some notes.

You would expect that after 6 years of war nobody would want to start another. Yet in the late 1940s it looked as if war might come to Europe again.

Do you remember (page 48) how the League of Nations tried to solve problems between countries? In 1945 the United Nations Organisation (UNO) was formed for the same purpose. Russia had worked with her western European allies in the war and everyone hoped this co-operation would continue. But it did not and in March 1946 Winston Churchill, speaking in America, said an 'iron curtain' had descended across Europe. This was of course not a real curtain. It was the boundary between the Communist lands controlled by Russia's dictator, Stalin, and those who wanted Europe to be free and independent.

Germany's old capital city, Berlin, was surrounded by land controlled by Russia. Britain, France and America all shared with Russia in governing Berlin. But in 1948 Russia refused to let any of their traffic cross her lands into Berlin. She hoped they would give in and leave Berlin to her alone.

Instead they organised a tremendous airlift to fly men and supplies of food and fuel into Berlin. Like this they went *over* Russian territory rather than *through* it. Look at Berlin airport above. See how each plane has a lorry parked by it. A loaded lorry is driving away. More empty ones are arriving. This went on, night and day, for 10 months, with a plane landing every 5 minutes. Then Russia lifted her ban. Why do you think she did that?

Because of Russia's behaviour, America, Canada and most of western Europe formed NATO – the North Atlantic Treaty Organisation. If an enemy attacked a NATO country the rest would come to her aid.

The Conservatives won the General Election of 1951 and Winston Churchill again became Prime Minister. Headlines in the newspapers said 'Winnie is back'.

Britain took several years to recover from the war. Ration books like these were used until 1954 and certain things were still scarce even after that.

Gradually we rebuilt our factories and houses. New towns were designed, like Harlow and Stevenage, with planned shopping centres free of traffic. What are the advantages of not having motor vehicles in a town centre? More and more towns now are closing at least some of their streets to traffic. Perhaps your nearest town has done this.

This is London in 1951. The Festival of Britain was held to make people feel proud of what they could do in peacetime. Look at:
— the loudspeakers through which cheerful music was played all day
— the trees and tubs of flowers
— the bright modern glass buildings
— the radar aerial on top of the tower, which bounced signals off the moon.

Eight million people visited the festival in 4 months. When it ended all the festival buildings were demolished except one. Find out which it was and why it was kept.

In 1955, when he was 80 years old, Winston Churchill retired as Prime Minister. The queen made him Sir Winston Churchill and a Knight of the famous Order of the Garter. He lived for 10 more years, still taking an interest in politics and world affairs. His long life had seen many changes. Much of it had been a struggle against the 'enemies of England'. When he died in 1965 the newspapers called him 'the greatest Englishman of his time'.

Huge crowds lined London's streets for his funeral. This boat is taking his coffin down the River Thames before it went to be buried in a village churchyard, near Blenheim Palace where he had been born.

**Things to do**

Here are just some of the many things invented or started in Sir Winston Churchill's lifetime:

| | |
|---|---|
| zip fastener | pedal bins |
| cigarette lighter | shopping basket on wheels |
| fountain pen | toothpaste in tubes |
| ball-point pen | stainless steel cutlery |
| safety razor | crossword puzzles |
| electric hair-clippers | neon lighting |
| rubber hot-water bottle | long-playing records |
| thermos flask | aerosols |
| wrist watch | plastics |
| detergents | man-made fibres, like nylon |
| electric light | self-service shops |
| launderettes | do-it-yourself shops |

You can find a lot more if you do some research. Design a chart or album about them. Try to find something about their invention from encyclopedias.

Try to find someone who went to the Festival of Britain exhibitions and ask what they remember about them. You may be able to borrow a catalogue or programme.

See if any of your relatives still have their old ration books or clothing coupons. Ask them to tell you how the rationing system worked and if it was fair.

# Index